Thou Shallt Love Thy Neighbor,

Thine Enemy And Thy God

Leslie D. Weatherhead

Kessinger Publishing's Rare Reprints

Thousands of Scarce and Hard-to-Find Books
on These and other Subjects!

- Americana
- Ancient Mysteries
- Animals
- Anthropology
- Architecture
- Arts
- Astrology
- Bibliographies
- Biographies & Memoirs
- Body, Mind & Spirit
- Business & Investing
- Children & Young Adult
- Collectibles
- Comparative Religions
- Crafts & Hobbies
- Earth Sciences
- Education
- Ephemera
- Fiction
- Folklore
- Geography
- Health & Diet
- History
- Hobbies & Leisure
- Humor
- Illustrated Books
- Language & Culture
- Law
- Life Sciences

- Literature
- Medicine & Pharmacy
- Metaphysical
- Music
- Mystery & Crime
- Mythology
- Natural History
- Outdoor & Nature
- Philosophy
- Poetry
- Political Science
- Science
- Psychiatry & Psychology
- Reference
- Religion & Spiritualism
- Rhetoric
- Sacred Books
- Science Fiction
- Science & Technology
- Self-Help
- Social Sciences
- Symbolism
- Theatre & Drama
- Theology
- Travel & Explorations
- War & Military
- Women
- Yoga
- *Plus Much More!*

We kindly invite you to view our catalog list at:
http://www.kessinger.net

Because this article has been extracted from a parent book, it may have non-pertinent text at the beginning or end of it.

Any blank pages following the article are necessary for our book production requirements. The article herein is complete.

THOU SHALT LOVE THY NEIGHBOR

Thou shalt love thy neighbor as thyself.
—Mark 12:31; Matt. 19:19; Lev. 19:18

THOU SHALT LOVE!" WE STOP THERE! OUR MINDS AT FIRST REJECT THE
words, for they seem to contradict one another. "Thou shalt!"
That is a command. A command is carried out by the will. We
can bend our will to any task we are commanded to do. We may
not succeed in it, but at any rate we can try. But to say, "Thou
shalt *love*," seems psychologically impossible. One cannot *love* to
order. Surely love is an emotion and beyond the control of the will.
Love rises up of itself without commandment or in defiance of
commandment, or it isn't worth calling love. Who, indeed, would
care to be the victim of someone's *commanded* love? Would it be
the real thing? Would it have the quality of the "divine emotion"?

Love, the theme of endless poets, artists, and musicians, is the
loveliest of all things that rise in the consciousness of man, the
most perfect flower his personality produces. It does not render
obedience to the will. It is called forth by the beauty and truth and
love around it. I am thinking not only of the love of lovers, but of
the love of friends. In the presence of one who really loves us our
minds find rest, our best is called forth, our ideals are shared;
wounds are not inflicted; they are healed. In the presence of the
loved person by whom also we are beloved we find the maximum
happiness, the deepest content, and a relationship entirely free from
fear. Such love provides infinite resource against the blows of the
hostile world outside; and when the world has done its buffeting,
such love is the harbor of the spirit, into which it steals like a bat-
tered ship from the troubled waters outside, to be equipped, re-
fitted, and refueled for the next voyage. Love is the gift of God,
the sharing of his nature, and the finest quality of human person-

ality. All this I think we mean when we use the word "love."

Surely, then, to say to a person, "Thou shalt love," is almost to commit the crime of seeking to bind two things together which are incompatible. It is like putting together a sword and a rose, a tank and a sonata, a steam roller and a little child's smile—the first, compulsive, forceful, driven by the will; the second, revealing a beauty born from above, kindled by a touch from God, breathing the very nature of the eternal world.

But the difficulty about our text is that it was *Jesus* who said, "Thou shalt love," who gave the commandment, indeed, high place, as the second of all the commandments—and Jesus "knew what was in man." He issued no commands in themselves impossible; and though we may say that the commandment runs back to the Mosaic law, nevertheless Jesus underlined it, reiterated it, and by his words about it gave it still greater authority.

We are driven, then, to suppose that the two are not incompatible; and since we cannot escape the imperious command "thou shalt," we must ask some very important questions as to what "thou shalt *love*" in the New Testament sense really means.

The main answer to this question will be a discovery that to "love" in the New Testament sense means a special way of directing the will. It does not mean that royal emotion we have been talking about. In a sense, it is a pity there isn't another word for it, for it must have confused many minds that Jesus should sanction the command "Thou shalt love." I shall ask you to remember this paraphrase of our text which I believe makes its meaning clearer: *Thou shalt adopt toward thy neighbor a sustained determination to show unbreakable good will in order that the best qualities in the person "loved" may be called forth.*

We had better go on to define the word "neighbor" also; and we shall remember that when Jesus was asked the question, "Who is my neighbor?" he promptly told the Jewish questioner a story about a man who was his traditional enemy, a Samaritan. I suppose if our Lord were still physically present, and a German asked, "Who is my neighbor?" Jesus would tell him a story about a Jew, or an Englishman. or an American; and if an Englishman asked, "Who is my neighbor?" Jesus would tell a story about a German, an Italian, or a Japanese. The meaning of the word "neighbor," therefore, according to the teaching of Jesus, is *anyone whom circumstance puts it in our power to befriend.*

Now let us turn to ask and try to answer the question: What is involved in "loving" our neighbor? And here I must say something in brackets. Whenever I preach a sermon that I think is rather original, whenever I express ideas that I have never seen in print or heard expressed anywhere else, somebody always comes up after the service and says: "Thank you very much for that sermon. *That is what I have always thought.*" Yet when one looks him in the eye, one knows that he is quite sincere. I think what happens is this: he means that ideas which have been lying in his mind and have never found articulate expression have suddenly been clothed in words for him—to his great delight. I felt the same myself recently. Returning from a preaching appointment in Cambridge, I bought Mr. C. S. Lewis' book *Christian Behaviour.* When I read it on the train, I was pleased and annoyed at the same time, for he says so many things that I have thought for a long time! And if now I say these things, you will accuse me of having cribbed them from Mr. Lewis.

I want to offer four points which I think are involved in "loving" our neighbor—two negative and two positive.

1. First, it doesn't mean "liking" our neighbor. Isn't that a relief? "Liking" is something that cannot be compelled. We like a person, or we don't like a person. Sometimes we like a person more if we know him better, but sometimes we like him less! I submit that it really would be impossible psychology to say: "Thou shalt 'like' thy neighbor." Let me repeat, therefore, that the emotion called "love" and the emotion of "liking" are not in the discussion. We are not commanded to feel affection for another. It is the *will* that is to be engaged, the will to show unfailing good will. In the Christian sense, we can "love" our neighbor without liking him, without having anything in common with him, and it would be

only intellectual dishonesty to pretend to "like" our neighbor, or to imagine that "liking" could respond to a command.

2. Second, "loving" our neighbor doesn't mean blinding ourselves to his faults. Obviously if the word "neighbor" is to be understood in the sense defined—namely, anyone whom circumstance puts it in our power to befriend—there may be very many things in the behavior of our neighbor which call forth our definite condemnation unless we are to lose our sense of ethical values. Suppose for a moment that we were thrust into the desperate situation of having to regard a murderer as a "neighbor." We should be bound to hate the beastly thing he had done, but we should still be asked by Christ to "love our neighbor"—namely, to show him a spirit of determined and sustained good will in order that his best qualities might find expression.

Receive, then, if you will, those two thoughts. Loving a neighbor does not mean necessarily "liking" him, and it does not mean overlooking his faults. That is what the old Christian writers inferred, I think, when they told us that we must love the sinner even though we hate his sin. Here Mr. Lewis has for us a very apposite word. He says:

For a long time I used to think this a silly straw-splitting distinction: how could you hate what a man did and not hate the man? But years later it occurred to me that there was one man to whom I had been doing this all my life—namely, myself. However much I might dislike my own cowardice or conceit or greed, I went on loving myself. There had never been the slightest difficulty about it. In fact the very reason why I hated these things was that I loved the man. Just because I loved myself, I was sorry to find that I was the sort of man who did those things.

Look back at our last two points in the light of that statement. We said "loving" is not a matter of "liking" and not a matter of blinding ourselves to faults. Isn't that exactly what we do about ourselves? Few of us, I imagine, really *like* ourselves. I find that, if I give an hour to honest introspection, I dislike myself for what I have done and for what I have been. Nor, I think, are most of us blind to our faults. We are blind to some of them because we know ourselves so incompletely. We all have many blind spots. But the more we do know ourselves and the more we see our own faults, the more we regard them with a great loathing. Yet disliking ourselves, and conscious of our faults, we go on "loving" ourselves in the sense defined. That is, we go on willing our own good. Moreover, we show a sustained determination in this matter; and nothing that happens, though we loathe it and hate it in ourselves, completely takes from us our belief in ourselves or makes us identify ourselves with the rotten things we do and are. The healthiness of this procedure is, I think, emphasized by our delight when, if we have been thoroughly bad-tempered, we overhear someone say, "He isn't quite himself today." We resent the thought of being identified with the meanness, unkindness, cruelty, and all the other kinds of unworthiness which we so frequently show.

Christ, therefore, is only asking that we shall do for others what we habitually do for ourselves—namely, refuse to identify them with the faults they exhibit, and adopt toward them that attitude of good will which rebukes the faults far more powerfully than condemnation, and is the kind of moral sunshine in which the virtues are made to blossom. In other words, "Thou shalt love thy neighbor *as thyself.*"

Now look at two positive things which loving our neighbor involves.

3. Our third point is that we must act *as if* we "liked" our neighbor. This is not a contradiction of our earlier point that we must admit we do not "like" him. Nor do I think it is a farce to try to act as though we liked him. When I search my own mind and examine my own attitudes to people, I find this: if I act as though I did *not* like them, I like them still less and find "loving" them in the Christian sense harder: if, on the other hand, I try to act as though I like them, I find I like them a little more and find "loving" them in the Christian sense easier.

Let me hasten to explain that by acting as though I liked my neighbor I do not mean that kind of servile ingratiation for which I think the slang expression "sucking up" is hard to beat. The man who "sucks up" to another person is not setting out to love others. He is setting out to make others love him, and some will go to any lengths, even surrender their own ethical judgments, rather than oppose the views and feelings of a person whose good will they are seeking to win. "Sucking up" is a neurotic symptom manifested either by those who have been starved of love, or those in whose nature childish fears of offending a grown-up person still sway their conduct even in mature years. "Loving" one's neighbor is not servile ingratiation. It is the sustained determination to show good will, and such determination is bound logically to express itself in acts. The acts will reflect the determination, but they will at the same time manufacture the emotion of liking.

One might express it by looking at the opposite. Not to "love" one's neighbor is to withhold good will. That increases the dislike, and the dislike is likely to be expressed in deeds which still further deepen the dislike and turn it into hate. If you hate people, you do yourself much harm—indeed, more harm than you can do to the person hated—and you will express the hate in cruelty and deepen the hate. In such an attitude you are widening the gulf between yourself and another, breaking the fellowship which it is God's plan to strengthen, and obviously you are landed in definite sin.

It is right to *hate* evil. No tepid disapproval is sufficient. It will not fire the energies of personality against that which must be ruthlessly fought. But let us not hate people. Let us believe in them. We hate only what evil people do, because we have seen a better way of life. If we hate the people who do evil, we shall never win them to doing differently; we shall antagonize them and make between us and them a gulf harder and harder to cross. Hate is a right reaction to evil but a wrong reaction to a person. To express the emotion of hate against evil is to purge the soul. To express the emotion of hate against a person is to poison the soul.

4. Our fourth point—the second positive one—is that we are helped to "love" our neighbor by remembering how God loves us. The sooner we part with the thought that God loves us because we are worth loving, or because of our moral achievements, or because of any of our qualities, the better.

Have you ever looked around a crowded bus and amused yourself with the whimsical thought that God actually loves all those funny-looking people? One can hardly withhold the thought: What funny taste God must have! They do look such a queer lot, and of course we look the same to them. Whenever I look at a crowd, I say to myself, "What queer taste God must have to love every one of these people!" And there isn't a person that he does not love. But he doesn't love us because we are clever or beautiful, or have a good figure, or a good brain. He loves us because we belong to him and because we are part of him. Indeed, if I may break into the subject of this sermon, his loving us is his only way of realizing his own God-ness. If he excluded you from his loving, he himself would be incomplete. In the two priceless parables of the lost sheep and the lost coin, both sheep and coin are quite content to be lost. The picture is that of the person who owns them dismayed by his or her sense of incompleteness, and the joy is the joy of a completeness recovered. God loves us as the poet or the artist loves that which he has himself created and which is part of himself.

We shall be helped to love others in the New Testament sense if we realize that God loves them, and that although God has the advantage over us in seeing perhaps lovable qualities in them which we cannot see, we are to act by faith where he acts by sight. Since we believe that there are lovable things deep in us—though the world may see few of them—we are to suppose that there are lovable things in everybody, and we are to act in such a way by sustained good will as to bring to obvious and glorious life the imprisoned splendors.

I love the familiar story of Michelangelo walking through the builder's yard and seeing in the corner a misshapen block of rough marble. When asked by the great sculptor what he was going to do with it, the builder said that it was useless. But Michelangelo made the famous reply: "It certainly is not useless," he said; "send it around to my studio. There is an angel imprisoned within it, and I must set it free." This will be the result of "loving" our neighbor. Sustained determination to show unbreakable good will is rewarded at last, I believe, by our being allowed to see from the unpromising natures of other men and women like ourselves the release of hidden beauty.

I have read somewhere that in the process of making the Kings-

way, which runs, as you know, between Southampton Row and
Aldwych, the excavations were so deep for the immense buildings
of that thoroughfare that soil was thrown up to the surface which
had not been exposed for many years. In that soil were seeds which,
it is alleged, the Romans must have brought over with them. I did
not know a seed could live so long. But, it is said, strange flowers
bloomed in that upturned soil, flowers never seen in England
before, though common enough in Rome. If the story is true, it is
another illustration of the kind of thing that happens when men
love their neighbors.

As I was writing down these thoughts, there came to my memory
the verse of an old hymn I had not heard since childhood. You may
know it:

> Down in the human heart, crushed by the tempter,
>   Feelings lie buried that grace can restore.
> Touched by a loving heart, wakened by kindness,
>   Chords that were broken will vibrate once more.

And with the memory of the verse came this most liberating
thought: there is no quality in any of the greatest saints that is not
present in every human life. Some qualities, perhaps, are as seeds.
The state of development may be immature. Some may feel that
the lovely things of life have become covered over, like the seeds
under the Kingsway, by the bricks and mortar of materialism and
even cynicism. But let me say it to you again: there is no quality
exhibited in the lives of any of the saints that is not present, at
least as possibility, in every human life. You may have a reputation
for being all kinds of things which men despise—mean or gossip-
loving, grabbing, conceited, or unclean—but you are also much
more than that.

The attitude of Jesus to men and women shows us how well he
himself fulfilled the command he lays upon us. Do you ask me
to believe that Jesus "liked" everybody? I wonder. With his insights he would see something to like which would elude us. But
I believe he "loved" everybody in the sense we have defined: that
he would adopt toward everyone a sustained determination to
show good will, and that, in doing so, he would call forth the best.

The flowers that had wilted and died, that seemed shriveled up and withered forever, would bloom again for him. To everybody else Matthew may have seemed a crusty old taxgatherer, and Zacchaeus a mean little moneylender. Neither of them seemed of any use to anybody. But in both cases deep under the soil were the seeds of saintliness. I wonder if Matthew knows today that in church we read from the Gospel according to *Saint* Matthew. If so, I think he smiles quietly to himself as he recalls the miracle of love which made his goodness blossom on the bleak soil of his earlier character. There was Mary Magdalene, her hair down on her shoulders, the sign of the prostitute, the woman of the street, spurned by everybody except one, who did not blind himself to her faults, for he said, "Her sins are many," and then added, "but she loved much." Indeed, I should imagine that often the harlot falls into the pit just because she loves much and wants to be loved, and, not finding the real thing, sells herself for a substitute love to those who "love" her body but stamp unheedingly upon the lovely things of the soul. One watches Jesus pushing away the rubble and stones and broken bricks, so that the seeds of the beautiful flowers of real love may have the wind and rain and sunshine of his friendship. He saved men and women like that. It was not his teaching; it was his loving. It was not the fulfillment of a ritual; it was just caring.

There cannot be the new world of dreams, can there, until in the New Testament sense we learn to love? And what a wonderful world it will be when men and women, frustrated and thwarted, cynical and unhappy, hating sometimes, indifferent sometimes, are brought through the grace of God to believe in one another and to love one another.

Some of you have said that you don't see any part that you can play in making the new world. I think the message of Jesus for today would not be that we should begin by "loving" the people in foreign lands, but that we might begin with the people in our own homes and in our own offices, the people whose lives touch ours every day. Everybody can begin there. You can.

"Thou shalt love thy neighbor as thyself."

THOU SHALT LOVE THINE ENEMY

Ye have heard that it was said, Thou shalt love thy neighbor, and hate thine enemy: but I say unto you, Love your enemies. —Matt. 5:43-44

THAT SOUNDS A VERY STRANGE TEXT TO ANNOUNCE, AND SEEMS A FOR-midable subject to discuss during wartime. You might even think it a dangerous subject and one likely to undermine the morale of our people. It might be easier conveniently to forget that Jesus ever said those words. I should not be at all surprised if someone felt immediately cynical, saying in his heart, "Do you expect us to love the Gestapo? Are you seriously asking us to love those who run concentration camps, persecute the Jews, lock up little children in filthy railway cars and send them to unknown destinations, tearing them away from their parents? Have you forgotten already the Nazi atrocities, the inhuman brutality, and authentic records of bestiality? The foul deeds of our enemies are proved beyond possibility of doubt, and you have the cheek to stand there in that safe pulpit and tell us to love our enemies. We bomb them night after night as hard as we can. Do you suggest that on an eight-thousand-pound bomb we should tie a label, 'With love from Britain'? Surely it would be better if you forgot these words for the time being. At any rate, I'm not going to listen to such nonsense."

If anyone feels like that, I entirely understand. It is a natural reaction to such a text. But since Jesus did say these words, and since it is sheer cowardice to put them in cold storage and drag them out again after the war, when perhaps it is easier to love the people of hostile nations, let us quietly think together about them, reminding ourselves of two important facts:

1. We shall not fight any better by hating people. Hate is an emotion which disturbs cool judgment and blurs good motives.

72

If those in command were moved by feelings of hatred of persons, they would speedily become unfit to command. Anyone who knows the British soldier can safely leave the matter of hate where it is. There is less hate shown among those who actually do the fighting than among those who stay at home, lose their loved ones, and are forced to remain inactive.

2. At this moment we are moved to a more generous mind because the war is going the way we want it to go. It is easier when we are winning to have a right attitude to those we are compelled to fight than when we are depressed or made savage by military reverses.

I can assure you quite sincerely that I am myself convinced that we must carry the war through to a successful conclusion. If there were a criminal band in our city, disturbing the peace, bringing sorrow and pain and suffering to innocent people, maltreating the aged and the poor, driving little children from their homes, prejudicing the peace and happiness of our city for years to come, then I think most of us would agree that that criminal band should be tracked down, punished, and its activities brought to an end. As I see the war situation, we are engaged in the same task, though the criminal gang is a large one and the methods we must use to bring the criminals to book are bound, in the nature of the case, to be far removed from the dispassionate mechanisms of justice which would accomplish the task in this one city. One of the most terrible entails of the attack of an international criminal gang is that the only way we can prevent it from having its evil way is the dreadful method we call war.

In dealing with the text "Thou shalt love thy neighbor" we made it clear that, since the word "love" is linked with a command, it cannot be a matter of the emotions, but must be a matter of the will. Let me remind you of what was said on that subject: When the New Testament commands us to love one another, the appeal is not to the emotion, but to the will. Romantic feeling is irrelevant. What is enjoined upon all who would call themselves Christians is a sustained determination to show unbreakable good will in order that the best qualities in the person "loved" may be called forth.

An emotion is not sufficiently within the control of the will. Therefore it would be nonsense to say to anybody, "Thou shalt love," if we were asking him to produce that warm emotion which generally goes by that name. "Thou shalt love" in the New Testament means, "Thou shalt adopt a sustained determination to show unbreakable good will." If you remember, it has been shown that loving your neighbor does not mean liking him, which again is a matter of feeling, not will; nor does it mean blinding yourself to his faults. It does mean acting *as if* you liked him, for acting *is* within the control of the will.

I want now to work out the same idea in regard to our new topic: "Thou shalt love thine enemy." It cannot mean liking our enemy, for no one could be expected to like the typical Nazi. Yet I do want to say that I not only like, but have a deep affection for, many friends I made in Germany. They have been silenced by Nazi tyranny and find no means of expressing themselves, but I am sure that they must hate the evil that has seized the high places of power, and that they still love and worship our Lord Jesus Christ. At the same time, no one who holds as precious the values for which we are fighting can possibly *like* those who have set themselves to destroy them, and who would fain practice a ruthless domination over the rest of the world.

Further, no one can possibly blind himself to the enormities that the Nazi regime has brought to literally millions of innocent people. In my view, the Allied governments are quite right in demanding punishment, in demanding that after the war, by legal courts duly constituted, those who are responsible shall be brought to justice. To say, "Thou shalt love thine enemy," does not mean letting him off. Such punishment will deal more charitably with the evildoer than the lawless revenge of Czechs and Poles would mete out to him.

We are now ready to try to express simply the positive implication of our Lord's words. Loving our enemy means acting toward him in the spirit of good will. Before you dismiss that as impossible while we keep fighting him and dropping bombs on his cities, let me show you two ways in which we still have to practice the spirit of good will, which is what the New Testament means by loving.

1. We must refuse to identify the crime and the criminal. I have tried to show how we must do that in regard to our neighbor, and how, indeed, we do it in regard to ourselves. When we have done something about which we are ashamed, we say to ourselves, truthfully and valuably, "That's not the real I," or, "l didn't realize what I was doing," or, "I'm ashamed of what I did"; and we are deeply relieved if somebody in charity says, "He couldn't have been himself." In other words, we make a separation between our real self and the things we do. Showing good will toward the enemy, that is, loving him, means a readiness to believe that the enemy is not expressing his real self in the foul deeds that he does. Years and years of evil teaching have made him accept false ideals. The inferiority which the crushing defeat of 1918 thrust upon him made him ready to clutch at any method of scrambling out of the abyss. The element of vengeance has swayed many German hearts, and Germany once more is trying to impose her aggressive, dominating spirit on the world. But hard though it may be to do so, we shall never make progress in the task of restoring good relationships after the war unless we can do, to some extent, what our fathers called "loving the sinner and hating his sin," that is, believing that the German is capable, as indeed he is, of making a contribution to the family of nations which is of immense value.

Some of us have studied German philosophy; others have studied German music; others again have read German literature; and still more have benefited by German scientific research, especially in the realm of medicine and surgery. I appeal to you never to identify the word "German" with all that is evil in the Nazi regime, but so to separate the evil from the people that have committed it that you are ready to show good will to the German, believing that what he has done in the past, in the way of contributions to culture, he may do in the future if only we do not identify him with the crimes of those who dominate him, and do steadfastly believe in his possibilities for good.

2. A second way in which we must show that good will to our enemies which Christ demands is by refusing to exaggerate their

crimes. As Christian people we must take a strong line here. Remember those great words of Paul in his first letter to the Corinthians, of which Moffatt has given us so excellent a translation: "Love is never glad when others go wrong; love is gladdened by goodness, always slow to expose, always eager to believe the best." One of the marks of a Christian is that he never exaggerates the evil of another. He admits it and is honest-minded about it. He doesn't whitewash it or pretend it never happened. But if a Christian gets one into a corner and almost licks his lips with satisfaction as he tells one the horrors that the Japanese or Germans have perpetrated, one knows that his Christianity is being undermined by the war.

Into the psychology of all this we need not enter now, but you will realize that to blacken another's character is to feel a little whiter oneself. We feel a little bit better when we have made others seem a little worse. The moral glow which a man feels when he reads in the newspaper of the fall of another is a glow he gets from the fires of hell, not from the stainless beauty of heaven. And anything which makes us feel, "I should never sink so low as that," rather suggests the machinations of Screwtape than the sanctity of the saints. The Christian attitude would be one of sorrow that members of a race—German, Italian, or Japanese—which has contributed so much to world happiness, and will continue to contribute so much more, could have been so deluded and bemused by those who have seized power over them as to do such unworthy and despicable things.

Let me summarize in one paragraph my message as I have developed it so far. Loving our enemies means a determination to show them good will. It does not mean liking them, or whitewashing them, or blinding ourselves to what they have done, or sentimentally refraining from punishing them. It does mean acting as though we still believe in them, and acting in two ways: (1) by not identifying the doer with the deed, as though they were inseparable—since we refuse to do that in ourselves—and (2) by refusing to exaggerate the evil in order to stir up hate or to feel better ourselves.

Now let us adopt a device which I have always found helpful in a difficult situation. When I am interviewing people in deep distress, people who ask the question, "What ought I to do?" I always test my advice by asking what would happen if they did the opposite. If, therefore, you are still critical of my repeating the words of Jesus, "Love your enemies," look for a moment at the opposite. If you decide that you cannot act toward the enemy in good will, then you will decide to act toward the enemy in bad will. If you don't "love" in the sense defined, you will hate; or, in other words, you will seek to bring about not ultimate good to the enemy—which I shall try to show in a moment is one of the great purposes of the war—you will seek to bring about ultimate evil.

You will be unable to seek ultimate evil for the enemy without hating him, and such hate is always a faulty psychological reaction.

> When I am dead. what I have guessed so long.
> My soul shall know in clearer, purer light:
> That where I loathed and hated, I was wrong;
> That where I loved and pitied, I was right.

The hatred of people is always a poison. I would commend, especially to my medical friends, the evidence contained in the book called *Disease and Integration,* by Dr. Newsholme, the medical officer of health for Birmingham, in which evidence is gathered and cases quoted to show that personal hate definitely manufactures toxins in the body.

I am not taking a lofty attitude of condemnation to the emotion of hate, as though I never entertained it myself. The tendency to hate people is a normal—and a non-Christian would say inevitable—result of the denial of desired love. If A loves B and wants all the love B can give him, and if B gives extravagant love to C, then A tends to hate both B and C. A hates B because he or she has given away love which A thinks belongs to him, and A hates C because C has been a party to the fraud by receiving the love which A thinks is his alone. It is very hard for A to stop hating both B and C. He can do it only by the grace of God, acknowledging meanwhile to himself the desire to hate and be revengeful. but acting as though he still loved both B and C, realizing that *if* he

gives vent to his hate, he will spoil his chances of attaining his
goal, that of winning love. He can win love only by giving love;
and if he cannot give the emotion, he must give the good will, that
is, he must love in the New Testament sense. Once he gives rein to
his hate, he will harm himself more than he can possibly harm the
person he hates. If, therefore, you say to me, "I shan't listen when
you tell us to love our enemies," I shall reply, "Beware of the opposite, for by hating you will harm yourself more than you can
hurt your enemies."

Further, this hate will bring about a permanent dislike, and the
dislike will mean that you steadily refuse to see any good at all in
the person hated. Once you do that to Germans as a whole, you
postpone the very thing for which we are fighting, a world of new
relationships. If we exclude Germany from this, we only sow the
seeds of another war in another twenty-five years. I should like to
bear witness, with pride, to the spirit of most British people, even
those who have lost their loved ones. There is nothing like the hate
in this country which I remember in the last war. During the last
war, in some places, German music could not be played at a reli-
gious service. People were commonly heard saying, "There is no
good German but a dead German." Such sentiments are rarely
heard today. Sometimes the emotion of hate sweeps over a person
who makes some such unguarded statement as I heard a lady make
in a train, that every German should be exterminated. But when I
suggested to her that she should be given a sword and invited to
start on a class of blue-eyed, golden-haired little German children,
her face told me that she would be the last to carry out her expressed
desire. The hate was in the emotional part of her mind for a moment. It had never gained access to her will or her thought. To hate
the enemy would be sin, for it would be making an unbridgeable
gulf in international relationships, while knowing that the purpose
of God is to make of all nations one family. It would be fighting
against God.

"But," you will say, "how can you use the word 'love,' even in
the New Testament sense of showing good will, when night after
night you are bombing the enemy?" Well, let's go back to the

earlier illustration of the criminal gang. Supposing, we said, that there were in this city a criminal gang, it would be the duty of the state to end its activity, even at the cost of human life. Granted that war is a faulty method of dealing with international criminals, yet—and the blame of this lies upon all our hearts—it is at present the only method of achieving the desired result. I hold, therefore, that it is justifiable. Though the method is a bad method, as compared with police activity in dealing with the crime of a city, the goal we have in mind may still be the same. Thus, the goal which the state has in mind is to make every criminal a good citizen. The goal the Allied governments have in mind is to make the Axis powers good neighbors. We desire the good of the enemy, though he himself, plus the sin of all the nations, has driven us to terrible methods of securing this end.

Let us make it clear to ourselves that the state, again and again, has to use a method which would be sin in the individual. For example, if somebody offended you personally, and you, with the help of a friend or two, tied him up in your cellar for six months, then I am afraid you would get into trouble, even though you could prove that you had fed him and given him some degree of comfort. Yet the state is rightly approved for passing a sentence of six months during which a man's liberties are restricted in probably a more austere way than the individual would adopt. In the same way, what would be murder in the individual may still be justified as the activity of the whole state, if it is the only way the state can find of achieving its end.

It may be that the state must even take life, and the Bible seems to me to approve that principle. For it is very important to point out that, when you read in the Old Testament the ancient command "Thou shalt not kill," you are reading in a bad translation. The Hebrew original means thou shalt do no *murder*, which is a very different thing. Murder is sin. It is an act in which the individual assumes an authority that may belong only to the state. And in the New Testament, when Jesus repeats the commandment, we find that the word used is not a word that means "kill," but "murder." Jesus does not say, "Thou shalt not kill." He does say, "Thou shalt do no murder." If the state finds that the taking of human life is the lesser of two evils—the other being the spread of international crime—if the taking of life is the only way by which an international criminal gang can be put down and the highest human values preserved, then I claim that the state has the right to take life, *and in doing so is not denying her purpose to show good will*—and to show good will is, in the New Testament sense, to love. Therefore there is no necessary conflict between loving your enemies and killing a sufficient number of them to make the rest desist in their attempt to spread evil.

Some of you may remember that shortly after the war broke out, when we were all trying to think our way through these things, I told a story of some Chinese pirates. I was rather amused afterward to find that somebody who heard me tell that story quoted it in Hyde Park as an answer to a pacifist speaker. The speaker, who is a great friend of mine, made fun of the story, supposing that I had invented it to substantiate my own argument. Actually it was not a made-up story at all. It was true, and if you turn up the files of the *Daily Telegraph* for February 2. 1935, you will find the details. What happened was this: Some British and American children were on board the steamer "Tungchow," on their way from Shanghai to school at Crefoo. They were set upon by pirates in the China Sea. With those facts in our mind, let us imagine that we were in charge of the children. If the pirates would not listen to reason, would not discuss the matter, would not do anything else than take the children off to their lair in the mountains for immoral purposes, do you think you would be justified in sending a radio message for a destroyer or an airplane? I am quite sure in my own mind that it would not be wrong to send such a message. Let us at once admit that it is wrong to risk drowning a pirate. But if your daughter of sixteen or seventeen had been on board, would you not feel it was a better thing to risk drowning pirates, or bombing them, than that an innocent girl should become a prostitute in a Chinese camp for perhaps a dozen years in some remote mountain fastness? In the actual case I am quoting the children were rescued by planes from the British aircraft carrier "Hermes," supported by the British destroyer "Dainty."

To my mind the international situation is not dissimilar. As we engage in war, there is no joy in our hearts at the terror and destruction it causes. For my own part, even the news of successful engagements gives me no feelings of hilarity, but only a kind of grim satisfaction that the end of the war is that much nearer. I have stayed in the Christian homes of some who lived in the area inundated by the floods released through the breaking of the dams in the Ruhr Valley. I think of one German Christian home in which I stayed for several happy days while attending a Christian conference. It consisted of a Christian father and mother, two girls, and a rosy-cheeked boy. Probably they were all carried away by a wall of water thirty feet high sweeping down upon them, and I am not ashamed to tell you that I cannot feel that it is a matter for rejoicing. All that one can feel, amid the conflicting emotions of sorrow, sadness, and grim acquiescence, is that probably only by such means can we save the remaining cities of Western civilization from the horror which befell Belgrade, Warsaw, and Rotterdam. One recalls, for example, that, *before war was declared on Holland,* and meeting with very little, if any, resistance, the Germans slaughtered thirty thousand people in Rotterdam, with not even the pretense of destroying only a military objective.

Again and again, life presents us with the difficult problem, not of deciding between the perfectly right and the obviously wrong, but of deciding the kind of question to which I have made reference. For example, shall the lives of the pirates be destroyed, or shall the British and American schoolgirls be made prostitutes? Even when one lifts the question to the highest court and asks what would Jesus do, there can be little doubt about the answer. For when we remember the perfection of Jesus, it does seem important to remember that Jesus was not a perfect man working in a perfect world, but a perfect man working in an imperfect world. If the former had been true, there would never have been moneychangers to turn out of the Temple, or proud Pharisees to receive the lash of his words. But Jesus was the perfect man working in an evil world, and could do only that which would achieve his end in the circumstances thrown up by evil. I feel confident, therefore, that the war must be prosecuted to its end and that we may even pray for the victory of our arms because, far from perfect though we may be, we have to use the only method to achieve our end which the evil in the world allows.

I know how deeply the thought of taking the life of the enemy troubles the consciences of some. I know how hopelessly inconsistent some feel it to be to talk about loving your enemy and trying to kill him at the same time. But think over this problem: Imagine that you yourself were about to commit the most horrible crime you can imagine yourself doing. I will not cite any imaginary horror, for there is no point in harassing your feelings. But then imagine that, before you committed this dreadful crime, you were shot. I wonder, if in the life to come, you would not be glad that you were shot before the crime was committed. You might even, in the next world, go up to the person who pulled the trigger and say, "Thank you very much. You did me a service." Jesus said a man was better dead than cruel to a child. This argument does not mean that you should go around shooting people here and there lest they commit a crime they will regret! Remember what we said about the state's being morally able to do that which is denied to the individual. But, in the light of the illustration, ask yourself the question again: Is taking life necessarily inconsistent with showing good will? I think it might be the highest expression of good will to Germany to stop her, even by killing, before bestial horrors have turned the whole world into a jungle. War, I claim, is not a denial of good will unless it makes you hate, and that is in your own hands.

I have referred in this sermon to enemies as though the Axis powers were the only ones. I must leave to you the application of the interpretation of the text in terms of your own personal and private enemies, but I will leave with you a picture which I saw lately in the press. A group of our men had been fighting fiercely and heroically in North Africa. They had been definitely trying to encompass the death of the enemy. Then, suddenly, the word went round that all resistance in North Africa was over and the campaign was ended. The very men who had been trying to encompass the death of the enemy are seen in a press photograph giving the same men—now German prisoners—chocolates and cigarettes. Now that is a parable.

As soon as the enemy ceased to be the personification of the evil we are trying to destroy, as soon as it became untrue to say that the only way of destroying the evil was to destroy the people who practiced it, as soon as the identification of evil with the people who committed the evil no longer needed to be made, then our determination to show good will was able to take a new turning, and our men are seen, not killing, but handing out chocolates. But please note this: *the determination to kill and the offer of chocolates came from the same motive,* the motive of good will toward the enemy. That good will had to express itself in killing first, because that was the only way of stopping the evil which the Nazi regime embodies. When that evil offered no further resistance, it was possible to separate the sin from the sinner, the evil from the people who *had been* doing it: and chocolates and good fellowship became the new expression of good will.

Such a picture made me wish that those who arrange the terms of peace should be those who fought the enemy. At the end of the last war we handed over the making of peace terms to politicians. I will make no comment on that save to say that the men who fought in the last war would never have imposed the terms which politicians imposed.

Love your enemies! Never let yourself hate! You may have a desperate task to break the evil which threatens the world, and the only way may be to fight and kill. But though we fight to the death, let us maintain unbroken good will and have the highest welfare of our enemies, as of the whole world, clearly in our minds, as the goal toward which we move. Those enemies also—possessed though they may be at present by evil demons—are the sons of the same Father who hates evil more than we do. but who loves all his children. When Jesus said, "Love your enemies," he added this: "that ye may be the children of your Father which is in heaven: for he maketh his sun to rise on the evil and on the good, and sendeth rain on the just and on the unjust."

A prayer that shows the true Christian spirit to our enemies was offered by the chaplain at the Sunday morning parade service on board the battleship "The Prince of Wales" on Sunday, August 10,

1941, at the historic meeting off the coast of Newfoundland between Mr. Churchill and Mr. Roosevelt, the meeting that gave us the Atlantic Charter:

Stablish our hearts, O God, in the day of battle, and strengthen our resolve, that we fight, *not in enmity against men, but against the powers of darkness enslaving the souls of men,* till all enmity and oppression be done away, and the peoples of the world be set free from fear to serve one another as children of one Father. who is above all and through all and in all, our God, for ever and ever. Amen.

THOU SHALT LOVE THY GOD

WE COME NOW TO THE THIRD OF THE TRILOGY OF SERMONS OF WHICH
the first was from the text "Thou shalt love thy neighbor," the
second, "Thou shalt love thine enemy," and now the third, "Thou
shalt love thy God." The order is not accidental. It is hard to love
one's neighbor. It is harder to love one's enemy. For many people it
is hardest to love God. In regard to the neighbor and the enemy,
we can put on them part of the onus of the difficulty of loving. We
can say, "My neighbor"—even if we use the term in the widest sense
—"is difficult. In any case I don't get on with strangers very well."
In regard to the enemy we can say, "It is particularly difficult in
these days to love one's enemy, and if I don't succeed, it is partly his
fault." But in regard to God we cannot put the onus on him. If
God is the perfect being and we fail to love him, the reflection is on
ourselves.

Yet I cannot feel that we are entirely to blame. On a lovely spring
morning, if health is good and spirits are high, and our loved ones
are near us and our relationship with them happy, and none of
them is ill or in danger, and we know of no people with whom we
are out of harmony, and business or professional cares are not
worrying us, then with Browning's Pippa we may go out into the
sunshine and say:

> God's in his heaven—
> All's right with the world.

It is easy then to tell ourselves that we do love God.

But there are days when God seems far off, vague, and unreal.
There are days when the spirit is half dead within us, and all the
wheels of being are slow; "when the burdens we carry chafe our
shoulders and weigh us down; when the road seems dreary and

endless, the skies grey and threatening; when our lives have no music in them, our hearts are lonely and our souls have lost their courage." There are days when the soul is stunned by bad news: illness threatens those we love better than life, or news of bereavement turns our hearts to lead and drives the sun from our sky. God's ways seem so confusing. It is hard to understand what he is doing and difficult to love him as one recalls the things that he allows. Many men, weighed down by the suffering and sorrow of the world, would confess that they do not really love God. If they were honest, they would say that they were critical about God and sometimes hostile to him. They are made unhappy only by being told that they *ought* to love him, for "ought" and "love" don't go together.

No true father says to his sons or daughters, "You *ought* to love me because I am your father," and it would be wise if we honestly recognized that in many families there is a good deal of insincerity in this matter of loving relatives. To suppose that brothers really love one another merely because they are brothers is to live in a realm of pretense. The frequent quarrels of sisters point the same way. Husbands and wives are frequently supposed to love one another, but in many a home love has given way to kindliness and to the desperate attempt to keep up appearances by making the best of a bad job. To call the relationship by the same name as that which binds two people who never chafe one another, always call out one another's best, find rest of mind and kindling of spirit in one another's company, wanting to do everything together and each finding himself or herself incomplete without the other, is indeed a misuse of words.

Those who carry out psychological treatments frequently find that relatives hate one another, and neurosis has often been set up by pretending to love and repressing feelings of antagonism and even hatred. Many a patient has suffered in childhood from some tyrannical and dominating parent who happens to have been labeled "father." Such a patient has never admitted to consciousness that she does not love him, because all the conventional shams of modern life and the Christian ideal she supposes she ought to hold conspire to tell her that she may admit to consciousness only the word "love," since the person concerned is her own father. Were he not her father, she would readily admit that she hates him and despises him, and she would find at any rate the beginning of some degree of health in labeling the emotion with honesty instead of with sham. Such a patient frequently breaks down at her father's death, especially if she has nursed him through a long illness. For she has a new conflict. She is really relieved and glad he is dead, but convention demands she should be sorry and show the signs of grief. She frequently develops the obsession that in some obscure ways she is responsible for his death. It is much more important for our mental health that we should be honest than that we should be conventional; and, as we said, "ought" and "love" don't go together. The teacher can say to the naughty schoolboy, "You *ought* to be sorry." If he could look into the schoolboy's heart, he would learn a good deal of psychology at once. He may proceed to cane the schoolboy, and then he does make him sorry, but he only makes him sorry that he was caned or that he was found out. To make him really sorry for the fault demands a different approach altogether. The only teacher who can make this approach is one who has an insight into the nature of things and who realizes at least the fundamental principles by which an emotional response of a true order may be evoked.

Now we always get a glimpse of the nature of God's ways with us by thinking about an *ideal* family. Jesus himself again and again argued thus from the ideal in man to the ways of God. The ideal father does not command that he be loved emotionally. He realizes that the fact of being a parent does not give him any right to demand love or even loyalty or even respect. These must be won. (In parenthesis, we often notice that a father realizes that he must win these things from, say, the little boy next door, and he sets himself out to do so when the little boy next door comes to play. But to his own little boy he is frequently brusque and demanding because he supposes his own boy *ought* to love him.) In the two previous sermons about loving our neighbor and our enemy, we found the key that opens the door. We said that, when we talk about loving our neighbor, the *feeling* of love is not meant, because an emotion cannot be commanded, but that loving means a determination to show unbreakable good will. When we talked about loving the enemy, the only way in which we could make sense of the command was to understand by it that we were to show the enemy an attitude of good will, and we proceeded to show that even fighting him might be an expression of that good will. For we are not fighting the German people as such; we are fighting the false ideas which have become their ideals, and with which at any rate the Nazi Party has so identified itself that the only way of overthrowing the ideas is to fight those who express them in their activities. Such fighting shows more truly an attitude of good will than a complacent indifference which allowed Nazism to spread over the world, to damn the souls of those who practiced it, and to victimize those who suffered through it.

When, therefore, the text says, "Thou shalt love the Lord thy God," it cannot mean, in my view, a feeling of warm emotion. That cannot, in the nature of things, be called forth by a command. What we have to show to God is good will. The father in the family, we said, cannot command emotion and, if wise, does not try to do so; but as the head of the family he has the right to command good will so long as his aims are directed to the welfare of the family as a whole and to every member of it. The family will fall to pieces if everybody is sabotaging the unity of the family and its purposefulness toward a high ideal. Thus the father has the right to say to his sons: "Do show me good will. Here are my purposes. These are my plans. This is what I am out for. Do co-operate with me. The unity of every family is essential in society. It is the basis of the happiness of the whole state. Don't, therefore, behave in a way that is hostile to those interests which we all have at heart." It would be a heavy father indeed who delivered himself of such a lecture to a young family, but, roughly speaking, I think that would be the attitude of an ideal father's mind. And I think that is the kind of thing God asks when in this commandment, which is underlined by the authority of Jesus, we are told to love the Lord our God with all our powers of heart and mind and soul, and thus of all our strength.

There will be many times, as we said at the beginning, when we have no warm emotional feelings about God; but, unless we are disloyal, there need not be any times when we sabotage his purposes and run our lives in opposition to his will. We may not be able to give God our feelings on many an occasion, but feelings do not matter, and feelings are not asked for. There need be no occasions when we cannot offer God our will and good will, and ask that, even on our dullest days, we may help, not hinder, his holy plans.

So to serve him by the offering of our will, even when feeling seems dead within us, is a truer expression of loving God than sitting in a deck chair in the garden *feeling* that we love God because the sun happens to be shining and the birds are singing, but never turning our hand to those great enterprises which we know to be his will. We are to love with all our strength. Strength is not expressed in feeling, but in the directed will. If that purposefulness is fired by feeling, so much greater the strength. But feeling alone doesn't get things done.

Even the phrase "loving with all our heart" is not, I think, an appeal to the emotions. Suppose that for twenty years you had set your heart on great literature, so that you knew the great poets and dramatists and prose writers and could quote them and communicate their magic to others. Suppose then, with a crowd of other people, you found yourself in a prisoner-of-war camp. The welfare officer sought you out and asked you whether you could give a few talks on literature to relieve the tedium of the other prisoners. I think you would be persuaded into helping. After all, literature is the thing you had *set your heart on*, not in feeling only, but in purposefulness. Your twenty years' enthusiastic study fitted you for a piece of service which no one else could give. Doesn't God say to us, "Set your heart on my kingdom, on the welfare of my world family. Study my ways with men; come into close fellowship with me. Then, when the moment comes, I can use you"? Emotion plays a part, of course, for it is impossible to separate thinking and feeling and willing. But loving God with all your heart does not merely refer to the flow of warm emotion. I think it means purposefully turning your whole being to the contemplation and study of God's ways with men, that, entering into the joys and delights of his kingdom, you may further his purposes in the world. As a boy sets his heart on stamp collecting, as a man sets his heart on being a great lawyer, as a girl sets her heart on being an able violinist, as a mother sets her heart on making her home a place of rest and recreation and renewal, let us set our hearts on the things of God and love him with all our hearts.

Loving God with our mind is such an immense subject that I hesitate to embark on it. It seems to me to mean a readiness to think things through with absolute honesty and untiring industry. I know that Christianity is a simple thing in one sense, but it is necessary that we should use all the powers of mind that God has given us to try to understand his ways with us. Fortunately, to be a good Christian one can be simple-minded and without high intellectual power. Indeed the man of simple faith often has insights into divine things that take him further than the theologian. At the same time, fearless and honest thinking would do a great deal for us, especially when we are confused and distressed by the things that happen to us. To have *thought out* a philosophy of life before calamity happens, as well as to "have faith," is to find shelter in the day of storm. Not to have done so, to have clung to an untruth or half-truth, even with much faith, is to find that the shelter breaks in upon one in the hour when one needs it most.

"Thou shalt love the Lord thy God with all thy mind." Thou shalt be willing to think things through. People hate to be made to think. In religion many seem to prefer magic and the mumbo-jumbo of meaningless words. Others seek to make themselves believe by repeating words instead of understanding them. But loving God with the mind means a fearless determination to follow truth wherever it leads us.

I was pulled up violently in this matter in India by a student with whom I attended a service during which the Creed had been recited, including the words, "I believe in . . . the resurrection of the body." He asked me what the words meant, and I replied that I meant by them a belief in the survival of personality after death. "If so," he replied, "why don't you say so?" The phrase "the resurrection of the body," if words are taken at their face value, means that the particles buried in the grave will be gathered again in some future state, and no one believes that now.

I am not making any cheap jibe at the creeds. They were set down, not to express final truth, but to combat immediate error. It is a matter for discussion whether they should continue to be used when, concerning their phraseology, one continually has to make mental reservations and odd interpretations involving making the words mean what those who wrote them down certainly did not mean. For everybody to say the same creed, but to mean something different by the words used in it, is to attain a spurious unity by a species of intellectual dishonesty. Some think the creeds should be restated every few years. Others argue that it is enough to keep the traditional words if modern explanations are made. But it is certainly wrong to allow room for so much misunderstanding that people hug words to their bosom when the strength of the truth has gone out of them. Many people today do not lack faith; but, not having been taught to love God with their minds, they "wander in perpetual twilight among shadowy ghosts of former faiths" which they do not really understand and cannot intellectually embrace, but which, for lack of clearer alternative, they cannot expel. In an attempt to rethink our way through Christian belief, we may have to reduce the number of beliefs very considerably, but it is better to have a few simple truths which carry intellectual conviction than to seek to embrace the whole theology of Christianity by mumbling words which we do not understand or cannot accept. I cannot help feeling that God loves the fearless, questing mind, even though there are many things which cannot yet be accepted because of the honesty of that mind.

"Thou shalt love the Lord thy God with all thy mind." Thou shalt not say words that mean nothing or mean something that cannot be accepted by the mind. Jesus opposed the hoariest traditions in order that he might satisfy the august claims of the truth. Somebody has asked what the condition of the nation's health would be if, in the days of Henry I, somebody had written down thirty-nine articles to be followed by all physicians for the rest of time. But our spiritual health is in peril partly because we are using words which the man in the street does not understand, which lead him astray if he takes them at their face value, and concerning which we have to give elaborate explanations which amount to admitting that the words mean something very different from what they say.

I must not attempt to work out all the meanings of loving God with the soul. I think it means turning our spirit to him, seeking to find harmony with him, being undismayed by the things that seek to lure us from him, never accepting defeat through sin, but turning back to him again in obedience and renewed dedication, and maintaining, by every means we know, our sensitiveness to his guiding voice. We may not have the ecstatic experiences of the mystics. We may not be very clever and be able to argue for our Christianity. I find that, more and more, it means for me putting one step down in front of the other, doggedly going on and trying to give God obedience and loyalty, setting my heart on the things of his kingdom, setting my will to obey his commandments and my mind to understand his ways and my spirit to look up to him in prayer. Feelings and mystic experiences are not for me to demand, as they are not in my power to engineer.

There is some kind of summary of my theme in the simple words of a song written by Maude Louise Ray:

> To love someone more dearly every day,
> To help a wandering child to find his way,
> To ponder o'er a noble thought, and pray,
>   And smile when evening falls;
>
> To follow truth as blind men long for light,
> To do my best from dawn of day till night,
> To keep my heart fit for His holy sight,
>   And answer when He calls,
>
> This is my task.

This is the end of this publication.

Any remaining blank pages are for our book binding
requirements and are blank on purpose.

To search thousands of interesting publications like this one,
please remember to visit our website at:

http://www.kessinger.net

CPSIA information can be obtained
at www.ICGtesting.com
Printed in the USA
LVOW13s0719250618
581791LV00030B/389/P